West Sussex Railways in the 1980s

Vic Mitchell and Keith Smith

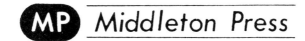

MP Middleton Press

*Cover pictures: Class H 0-4-4T no. 263
bursts through Ketches Bridge on the
Bluebell Railway in April 1982 and
Chipman's weedkilling train approaches
Arundel station on 2nd June 1989, on its way
from Norwood Junction to Bognor Regis.
The locomotive is no. 20904.
(B.C. Skelton and C. Wilson)*

As part of its fund raising for the Scanner Appeal the Chichester Health Authority organised a railway photographic competition, in conjunction with the Observer Newspapers and Middleton Press, during the summer of 1989. Many of the entries are included in this volume and the winning pictures in the four classes are indicated accordingly. The appeal will also benefit from sales of this book and readers wishing to support further this project can do so via the publishers.

First published November 1989

ISBN 0 906520 70 3

Copyright - Middleton Press, 1989

Design - Deborah Goodridge

Laser typeset by Barbara Mitchell

*Published by Middleton Press
Easebourne Lane
Midhurst, West Sussex
GU29 9AZ
Tel. (0730) 813169*

*Printed & bound by Biddles Ltd,
Guildford and Kings Lynn*

CONTENTS

ACKNOWLEDGEMENTS

We are grateful to all those who entered the Scanner Appeal photographic competition and to its organisers, B. Boxall and P. Hounsome. Also, we are very appreciative of the assistance received from C. Attwell, D. Cullum, N. Langridge, D. Smith, E. Staff, N. Stanyon, A. Whitehart and our wives.

INDEX

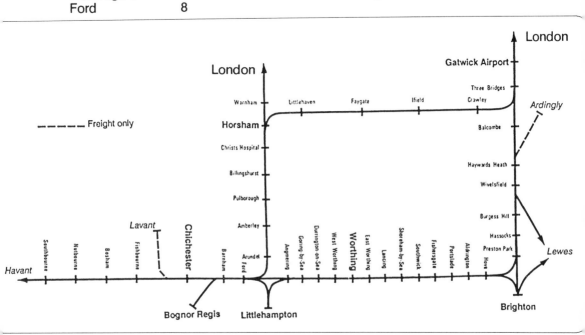

HISTORICAL BACKGROUND

The first passenger railway in the county, between Brighton and Shoreham, was opened on 12th May 1840 and this was followed by the main line to London Bridge, which was completed on 21st September 1841. The route west of Shoreham reached Worthing on 24th November 1845, Ford on 16th March 1846, Chichester on 6th June 1846 and Havant on 15th March 1847.

The branch from Three Bridges to Horsham came into use on 14th February 1848 and was extended to Petworth on 15th October 1859. The link between Pulborough and Ford had to wait until 3rd August 1863. The branch to Littlehampton followed two weeks later and that to Bognor came into traffic on 1st June 1864. The history of the secondary lines of the county are described in detail in other publications.

Electrification of the route between Three Bridges, Brighton and West Worthing took place on 1st January 1933, while the other passenger lines included in this album had to wait until 2nd July 1938. For promotional reasons, BR changed the route descriptions; in 1972 the former LBSCR West Coast line became "Coastway West" and the Mid-Sussex line became the "Arun Valley Line" in 1986. Its northern limit is officially Horsham, but this term is now commonly used to describe the route as far as Crawley. We will do likewise in this album.

The organisation of BR was changed fundamentally in 1986, when business sectors were formed, such as InterCity, Provincial, Network SouthEast (NSE), Parcels and Railfreight, the latter having several sub-Sectors.

A further development took place in May 1989 when the electric services in this area were put under the marketing banner of "Sussex Coast Lines".

SIGNAL BOXES

Brighton Box was damaged by fire on 1st October 1984 and was closed completely on 29th April 1985, when Three Bridges Panel took control of the area. By the end of the decade, this panel, together with those at Arundel and Lancing, controlled Coastway West between Brighton and Barnham.

The principle signal box closures are listed below, but some had been down graded to gate boxes prior to closure.

11 July 1983	Three Bridges
	Haywards Heath
	Keymer Junction
17 March 1984	Preston Park
	Hove
1 December 1985	Woodgate
	Drayton
	Whyke
20 April 1986	Crawley
	Faygate
14 May 1988	Portslade
	Shoreham A & B
4 June 1988	Worthing
	West Worthing
25 June 1988	Goring
	Angmering

A notable signalling development was the introduction of reversible running on both tracks between Keymer Junction and Preston Park in March 1985.

GEOGRAPHICAL SETTING

The northern part of the county is situated in the Weald, which is predominantly clay. This is separated from the coastal plain by the chalk mass of the South Downs, through which the London-Brighton main line passes by means of a series of tunnels, while the Arun Valley line makes use of the Arun Gap.

The gravel of the coastal plain gives rise to substantial rail traffic at its western end, in the Chichester area. Brighton is at its eastern end, the station being about 100 ft above sea level. This results in westbound trains having to descend to the plain, while northbound services climb to the tunnels through the Downs.

PASSENGER SERVICES

For the sake of brevity, the services are
described in one direction only.

Coastway West and Arun Valley

In 1980, the basic hourly service comprised -

Brighton - Portsmouth semi-fast
Victoria - Bognor Regis via Arundel and Littlehampton
Victoria - Portsmouth (via Arundel. Bognor Regis
 portion detached at Barnham)
Victoria - Littlehampton via Hove
Brighton - Portsmouth all stations
Brighton - Bognor Regis all stations via Littlehampton

From May 1984, this was amended to -

Brighton - Portsmouth all stations, connecting with -
 Littlehampton - Bognor shuttle
Brighton - Littlehampton all stations
Brighton - West Worthing all stations
Victoria - Portsmouth via Hove (where a stopping
 portion to Littlehampton was
 detached)

Thus Chichester and stations west lost their
regular direct service to the Arun Valley,
which itself no longer had two trains each
way, each hour, although Horsham retained
a half-hourly service to London.

Since May 1986, the Victoria - Portsmouth
service has detached its Littlehampton
portion at Worthing, instead of Hove.

Coastway West, since May 1988, has
benefitted from the introduction of several fast
trains on weekdays between Brighton and
Portsmouth, calling only at Worthing,
Chichester and Havant, although a stop at
Barnham was added a year later. Hopefully,
such commendable improvements will
continue, despite insufficient publicity.

Brighton Main Line

The decade opened with a normal hourly
timetable between Brighton and Victoria of
one fast, one semi-fast and two stopping
trains. In 1981, one train each hour was
diverted to London Bridge and since May
1988 it has been extended to Bedford via the
Thames link route.

Through services to the West

After an alarming decline in through trains
in the 1970s, Bristol and Exeter trains were
available in 1980, although only on Saturdays.
In 1981, a Sundays only Cardiff service was
added. Further improvements were noted in
the summer of 1982, when the Exeter trains
was extended to Paignton. From May 1983,
it was possible to travel to Penzance without
changing, but only on Fridays and Saturdays

A useful through train was provided between
Portsmouth and Newhaven Harbours in the
summer of 1986, but only one journey on
weekdays. Sadly the enormous benefit (to
BR and to passengers) of a frequent through
service along the entire Sussex Coast is yet to
be realised.

The return trip to Cardiff has been operated
daily since May 1984 and twice daily since
May 1988, one train originating from Milford
Haven.

Since May 1989, the Saturday and Sunday
Plymouth train has operated via Portsmouth
Harbour, where reversals adds 25 minutes to
the journey.

Through services to the North

After a long absence, through trains north
were restored in 1979, with two to Manchester
daily. One of these was diverted to Liverpool
in 1983. In 1984-86, the weekday service
comprised two trains to Manchester and one
to Derby. From May 1986, there was one
Manchester and two Liverpool trains and
twelve months later this was amended to
three and one respectively. Since May 1988,
the timetable has shown one train to
Manchester and one to Edinburgh, the latter
being named "The Sussex Scot".

COASTWAY WEST

1. No. 47447 is seen on the Cliftonville Curve with the 08.50 Hove - Manchester, service on April 17th 1985. The curve links the Coastway West with the main line to London, the Brighton - Hove lines being visible in the background. Due to the Brighton Signal Box fire, all loco hauled trains started from Hove or Gatwick, until the full resignalling was complete. (J. Petley)

3. Although long closed to general traffic, Hove goods yard continued to handle domestic coal throughout the 1980s, the mechanised facilities being visible on the left. Electro-diesel no. 73107 slumbers in the sun on the 17th August 1989. (V. Mitchell)

2. Hove down side continued to present a pleasing mixture of architectural styles; the part on the right dating from 1865, that in the centre being 1893. The vaulted canopy was removed from Victoria station in about 1905 and is seen here in 1982. (J. Scrace)

4. Aldrington lived up to the hopes of its Edwardian constructors and was still busy in the 1980s. The SR rebuilt the platforms in concrete and BR dropped the suffix "Halt". (J. Scrace)

5. The westward view of Portslade in March 1982 was little changed in 1989, apart from the loss of the sidings and the signal box. A threat to demolish the buildings in the mid-1980s was averted. (J. Scrace)

6. Unit no. 6053 halts at Fishergate on 14th April 1982, bound for Brighton. The electrical equipment in the background handled the output from Shoreham Power Station, which was closed and demolished at the end of the decade. (J. Scrace)

7. Between May 1987 and May 1989, the only locomotive hauled train on Coastway West was the Exeter service, which ran on Saturdays only. No. 47557 has just passed through Southwick (visible in the background), with the 05.47 Exeter - Hove on 21st May 1988. The train returned at 11.05 from Brighton. (J. Petley)

8.   Ex-Metropolitan Bo-Bo locomotive no. 12 *Sarah Siddons* crosses the River Arun near Ford, with the Sarah Siddons Railtour returning from Portsmouth to Victoria via what was then still known as the Mid-Sussex line. The date is 7th July 1984. (C. Wilson)

9. Seen in 1982, the up signals west of the Worthing level crossing carried "calling-on" arms, marked "C". These enabled the second portion of London-bound trains to enter either up platforms, to join the front part already standing there. (J. Scrace)

10. Early opulence at Worthing - the Star of David cast into the down platform canopy supports. Contemporary economy - the parcels office sign, lettered on the other side only. The date is 2nd January 1983. (N. Langridge)

11. To the left, preparations are in hand to remove the semaphore signal and reveal a colour light behind. In the centre of the picture is the late running Milford Haven to Brighton Sprinter service. To the right, an EPB is stranded in a gap in the conductor rails at the entrance to West Worthing EMU sheds on 4th June 1988. (P. Barnes)

12. On Sundays in 1986, the Cardiff service departed from Brighton at 16.12. It is seen at speed near Angmering on 7th September, behind the now withdrawn no. 33210. (J. Petley)

13. F&W Railtours "Coastway Crusader" departs from Littlehampton behind 25191 and 33011 and heads for Wolverhampton on Sunday 27th July 1986. The carriage washing machine in the background was out of use for much of 1989, due to water shortage. (C. Wilson)

14. A view from Littlehampton station on 18th April 1987 showing the new track bed laid during the previous night. The engineers had occupation of the site for the entire Easter weekend, EMUs being stabled at various locations in the district. (C. Wilson)

15. The 14.00 Victoria to Bognor Regis service is seen at platform 3 at Barnham on 23rd September 1981. Use of the adjacent carriage sidings declined subsequently and they eventually became redundant. (J. Scrace)

17. The goods yard at Barnham closed on 28th September 1964 but part of it was retained for use by the Permanent Way Dept. and is visible on the right. The 10.03 Chichester - Victoria service arrives on 28th August 1982. (J. Scrace)

16. On the 17th August 1982, the coaches used on the British part of the Venice-Simplon-Orient Express were hauled by no. 73142 to Bognor Regis. Barnham signal box is visible above the second coach. Upon arrival at Bognor Regis, the BBC renamed the station Folkestone Harbour and commenced filming. (J. Scrace)

18. The massive gasholder was a landmark north of Bognor Regis until the end of 1989. The gasworks siding was taken over by LEC Refrigeration in 1964 and was in use until 1972. The right hand signal post controlled access to the goods yard until 1971. Relaying is seen in progress on 24th November 1984. (C. Wilson)

→

19. Bognor Regis terminal buildings date from 1902 and were beginning to show their age when photographed in 1981. Demolition proposals in 1989 were greeted by fury in the town and its salvation now seems likely. (J. Scrace)

20.   The 10.36 Bognor Regis - Littlehampton passes the all-mechanical signal box on 21st August 1982. The three carriage sidings are in the background. (J. Scrace)

21.   On the same day, no. 3203 stands at platform 1, no. 7433 at no. 2, while no.3 is empty. No. 3 can receive loco hauled trains, as a crossover allows the engine to be released via the middle track. (J. Scrace)

22. A blizzard rages at Bognor Regis on 6th February 1986, as no. 7361 departs from platform 2 for Victoria at 12.04. All platforms, except no. 4, can accommodate twelve coaches. (C. Wilson)

Diagram of the sidings east of Chichester

1. To Chichester
2. Bartholomews' siding (agricultural)
3. Chichester bypass A27
4. Cory's siding (domestic heating oil)
5. Gravel discharge bridge
6. Drayton Crossing
7. To Barnham

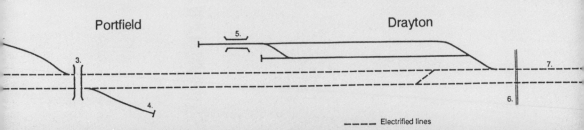

Portfield   Drayton

Electrified lines

23. Headcode 99 was used for Bristol and Cardiff services, 11 being applied to Exeter trains. No. 33052 waits at Chichester on 21st August 1988. On the left , cars park on the site of the Midhurst bay, then recently infilled. The down bay has lost its track but retains its number. (V. Mitchell)

24. The great storm on 17th October 1987 felled thousands of trees and as West Sussex was the most wooded county in its path, their disposal presented an enormous task. Chichester despatched a train load almost every working day until June 1989. No. 33013 prepares to depart west on 4th February 1988. (V. Mitchell)

25. The electrically operated crane in Chichester goods yard was one of the last SR structures of this type to remain standing. It was dismantled in 1987, after having been out of use for many years. (P. Hounsome)

Chichester & Midhurst Railway

A society was active in the late 1980s, planning to reopen this route for steam train operation, when BR ceases to use the line to Lavant. The scheme was amended to cover the part south of Singleton, but despite encouragement from some local authorities, opposition has been encountered from residents unaware of the minimal impact of a railway on the environment.

26. Since 1972, unwashed gravel has been transported from Lavant, two miles north of Chichester, to the processing plant at Drayton, a similar distance to the east. Having passed under the new bridge west of Chichester on 3rd June 1988, no. 73117 *University of Surrey* hauls the special wagons eastwards along the goods loop, which has conductor rail as far as the eighth wagon. (C. Wilson)

28. InterCity liveried no. 73136 runs round its gravel train at Brandy Hole Lane, north of Chichester, before propelling it to loading hoppers at Lavant on 10th March 1986. (C. Wilson)

27. The Ardingly to Whatley Quarry empty stone train often consists of 37 wagons and has a reputation for causing locomotive failures. It also causes antagonism here at Chichester when it stops for crew changing and blocks the level crossing. Unnecessary delays to ambulances and the fire service could be catastrophic. It is running west, past the new link road and sports centre, on 30th June 1988. (C. Wilson)

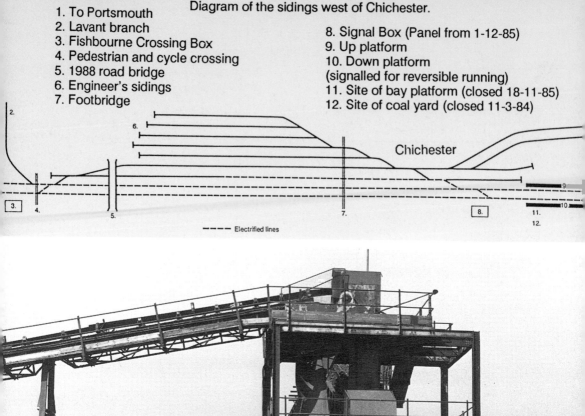

Diagram of the sidings west of Chichester.

1. To Portsmouth
2. Lavant branch
3. Fishbourne Crossing Box
4. Pedestrian and cycle crossing
5. 1988 road bridge
6. Engineer's sidings
7. Footbridge

8. Signal Box (Panel from 1-12-85)
9. Up platform
10. Down platform
(signalled for reversible running)
11. Site of bay platform (closed 18-11-85)
12. Site of coal yard (closed 11-3-84)

Chichester

- - - - - Electrified lines

29. At Lavant, the empty train is propelled into a tunnel, above which the gravel is stockpiled, and is loaded in two stages by an employee of the gravel firm, Tarmac. A long (and ever lengthening) series of conveyer belts bring the material from the working face. No. 73134 *Woking Homes* prepares to pull forward on 22nd September 1986. (V. Mitchell)

31. Following the opening of the bridge, seen in picture 26, Fishbourne Crossing was only available to cyclists and pedestrians. Plans were made for a light controlled crossing that would pass over three tracks instead of two, as the Lavant line would once again have its own separate track. (V. Mitchell)

30. To mark the centenary of the opening of the line between Midhurst and Chichester, your authors planned a number of events on 11th July 1981. One of these was the operation of DEMU no. 1126 (by the area Woking Homes Committee) on the remaining part of the line towards Lavant. One of several trips is seen returning to the junction by Fishbourne Crossing. (D. Dornom)

32. Almost within sight of the junction is Clay Lane Crossing, seen in April 1984 with its resident keeper, Mrs Ivy Welsh, in action. She subsequently retired but the gates were still hand operated in 1989. (V. Mitchell)

———————————▶

34. Having just passed over Blackboy Lane Crossing, an eastbound freight service runs through Fishbourne on 18th April 1984. In December 1987, a £2 million scheme was announced to modernise the crossings and signalling between Chichester and Havant, some work having been started during 1989. (V. Mitchell)

33. More hand worked gates were to be found beyond both ends of the platforms at Fishbourne. This eastward view in April 1989 includes another new road bridge, this one carrying the re-routed A27 trunk road, which now links the Chichester and Havant bypasses. (J. Scrace)

35. No. 33030 passes Bosham with a ballast train en-route to Chichester yard on 27th January 1989. This was in connection with engineering works between Chichester and Barnham during the coming weekend. This was the last signal box on the Coastway West to have a gate wheel and a complete set of semaphore signals. The most westerly station in West Sussex is Southbourne and that had its gates converted to lifting barriers on the 4th December 1988, temporarily controlled from the nearby signal box. (C. Wilson)

36. Class 155 Sprinters were introduced on the Cardiff - Brighton services in May 1988 and, due to door defects, were replaced during the following December by the superior class 156 units. The 05.47 from Milford Haven has just passed Fishbourne Junction on 15th September 1988. Sprinters presented the only example of Provinicial Sector livery in the county. (C. Wilson)

37. No. 33029 removes another load of fallen timber from Chichester as it runs west along the bi-directional goods line. The wood was mainly destined for South Wales and Scotland, but some went to Italy via the train ferry. (P. Hounsome)

38. There have been frequent clashes of livery in the 1980s, such as the coupling of the patriotic NSE colours to the earlier and more popular "Jaffa cake" style. This was as short lived as an earlier BR edible colour scheme - "plum and custard". (C. Wilson)

39. *A loaded gravel train of about 1000 tons gross passes the former railway cottages at Fishbourne, hauled by no. 73117 UNIVERSITY OF SURREY. These trains invariably travel along the goods line in perference to the up main. (P. Hounsome)*

40. A look back along Coastway West in colour, shows the scene before and after the paint splashing NSE came into existence in 1987. A Portsmouth Harbour to Victoria service runs into Barnham on 6th April 1985. (R. Dorkings)

41. At Barnham in May 1989, a Trac-Gopher was photographed. This uncommon peice of equipment has an extendable rotary cutter of value in digging drainage ditches and removing ballast in restricted spaces. (G.E.Teague)

42. The concourse at Bognor Regis retains its original character and traditional barriers although the booking hall has been totally de-humanised. On the left is the charming vaulted entrance to the buffet. Redevelopment plans involve the erection of a new station on the platform area, the old buildings being demolished or redeveloped. They received a Grade II listing in August 1989. (P. Hounsome)

43. Rebuilding of Littlehampton station started in 1937 when a temporary structure was provided. After numerous changes of plan, new buildings finally came into use in 1987. They had considerable more style than the cubes which were erected in the previous decades. (C.N. Cheney)

44. Driver Alec Lovell waits with Saun Morris on 29th August 1986, the BI indicating that his unit is based at Brighton. The leading 1st class compartments in these sets are being downgraded when they are repainted. (R. Dorking)

45. *Two DMU units made an unusual sight at Littlehampton on 9th July 1988. These were returning to Aylesbury, via Brighton. (R. Dorking)*

46. *The Hollycombe Steam Collection was open on Sundays and Bank Holiday afternoons from Easter to the Autumn, throughout the 1980's. The 2ft gauge Barclay 0-4-0WT CALEDONIA is being admired on 3rd May 1981, the signal behind it being on the standard guage line. By 1988, JERRY M, a Hunslet 0-4-0ST of 1895, was also at work in this senic location on the West Sussex border, south of Liphook. The standard gauge geared 0-4-0T SIR VINCENT moved to Rushden, Northants, during the summer of 1989. (A.G. Storey)*

47. *The Chalks Pits Museum at Amberley has a very extensive collection of industrial railway equipment of various gauges on exhibition. Bagnall 2-4-0T POLAR BEAR is seen near its shed in July 1987, devoid of its large brass dome cover. The 500 yard long demonstration line was officially opened on 5th June 1984. (D. Mark)*

48. *The scene in July 1989 includes the French built 0-4-0T BARBOUILLEUR and a Wingrove & Rogers battery-eletric mine locomotive. By then, POLAR BEAR had retired with defects in its marine boiler. (D. Mark)*

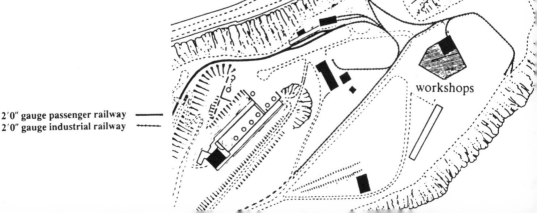

2'0" gauge passenger railway ——————
2'0" gauge industrial railway +·+·+·+·+·

workshops

49. Bluebell Railway staff confer in May 1980 in uniforms which represent the highly professional standards acheived on the line. While BR standards improved during the decade, many individuals could improve their presentation, particularly regarding footware. (D. Mark)

50. Pictures nos. 50 to 63 show the remarkable acheivements of the staff and volunteers on the Bluebell Railway in the restoration and maintenance of their diverse range of railway equipment. Here the 1877 Fletcher Jennings 0-4-0T BAXTER receives attention in May 1981, it subsequently being available for shunting until 1988. (B.C. Skelton)

51. The fireman struggles with "the bag" as Adams 4-4-2T no. 488 is refreshed on 15th May 1988. After a period in BR black, it is seen back in LSWR colours at the age of 103. (A.G. Storey)

CLASS D - PRIVATE RAILWAYS

52. *Schools class no. 928 STOWE waits for Terrier no. 72 FENCHURCH to arrive at Sheffield Park on 25th August 1985. The leading coach is the ex - GNR director's saloon.* (A.G. Storey)

54. *The setting sun in November 1988 found no.55 STEPNEY in a temporary livery, applied on an advesive material, for the "Hayling Island" day. This engine was the first to run on the revived line, back in 1960.* (S. Edbeare).

53. No. 72 was piloted by P class 0-6-0T BLUEBELL and sister Terrier no. 55 on Freshfield Bank on 13th July 1985. As the carriage shed is at the north end of the line, it is often convenient to couple locomotives together to fetch their trains. (D. Mark)

55. *The southern terminus of the Bluebell Railway is seen, authentically finished in the LBSCR colour scheme. Horsted Keynes is equipped and painted to represent the SR era and, since it is in East Sussex, it may be included in a future companion album. (D. Mark)*

56. USA 0-6-0 T no. 30064 climbs Freshfield Bank, during the special weekend to commemorate the return to steam of *Stowe* on 13th June 1981. The short wheelbase of no. 30064 gives the crew an uncomfortable ride. It has been out of traffic since 1985. (J. Petley)

57. Adams Radial Tank no. 488 is also seen on Freshfield Bank, on 31st August 1980, prior to its second major overhaul in Bluebell ownership. It returned to traffic for its centenary in 1985, when it was fitted with its original style of stovepipe chimney. (J. Petley)

58. Merchant Navy class **Port Line** arrived on the Bluebell Railway after being exhibited at the LSWR 150 event at Woking in May 1988, following a lengthy restoration programme. It is on loan prior to eventual use on the Swanage Railway and is seen near Farm Bridge on 28th May 1989. (J. Petley)

59. On the cold afternoon of 21st February 1982, class Q1 no. 33001 storms up Freshfield Bank with an assortment of the line's beautifully preserved coaches. The locomotive is on loan from the National Railway Museum but has been out of use since 1985. (J. Petley)

60. BR standard class 4 no. 75027 was in use for most of the 1980s, finally being withdrawn in September 1989 for its boiler to be lifted from its frame, for the ten year inspection. It is seen on 7th May 1983, passing close to the site of the future Ketches Halt, opended in May 1989. (J.Petley)

61. No. 80064 was built at Brighton in 1953 and has been in use on the Bluebell Railway since 1984, after working for a while in Devon. It is steaming well on 19th June 1988, close to Freshfield Halt which was closed at the end of the previous season. (J. Petley)

62. SR no. 21C123 was BR no. 34023 (*Blackmoor Vale*) and is the only example on the Bluebell Railway of a Bulleid Pacific in its original condition. It emerged from Brighton Works in 1946 and is seen on 14th June 1981. Sadly it has not moved since 1985, when its boiler insurance expired. (J. Petley)

63. We make no apology for including so many classic three-quarter views of steam trains, since they are *classic* locomotives on a *classic* preserved railway. Ex-SECR no. 592 gleams on 1st June 1980, with ex-Kings Cross suburban coaches, now on Tyneside. Once one of a class of 109, this sole survivor has been under repair since 1984. (J. Petley)

64. A fine minimum-gauge railway is operated less than one mile west of Pulborough station. An East African type 4-4-4 is pictured on 25th May 1987, on track which was doubled in 1989. (V. Mitchell)

ARUN VALLEY

65. The new station for the new town of Crawley is pictured in 1982, but by 1989 the concrete cladding of the office block was spalling and passengers on the up platform had to be protected from falling fragments by scaffold boards. (J. Scrace)

67. Although rostered for two class 73s this Horsham - Three Bridges engineers' train was provided with nos. 33060 and 33051 on 11th July 1983. They are seen near Ifield. (J. Petley)

66. Due to the line being shut between Three Bridges and Haywards Heath, Inter-Regional trains in February 1983 terminated at Gatwick, with the stock running to Horsham for servicing. No. 47468 passes snow covered Crawley on 12th February 1983. Class 47s are very rare on this line as they are not permitted south of Horsham due to bridge weight restrictions. (J. Petley)

68. During the early morning of 17h October 1987, the great storm devastated West Sussex and threw hundreds of trees onto the tracks. By mid-afternoon, a few trains were moving, indluding this DMU which left Horsham at 15.21 and is seen passing through Faygate. (P.G. Barnes)

70. Littlehaven retained its gates longer than most places on the route, as the road required extensive re-profiling, as seen here on 26th June 1986. The mirror for the signalman is also visible. (V. Mitchell)

69. Class 501 units normally worked on the North London line but on 11th May 1985, two sets operated the "Farewell Tour" before being withdrawn. They are passing the hybrid signal box/booking office at Faygate - the box closed in April 1986 and the office ceased to be staffed in October of 1987.
(J. Scrace)

71. The VSOE coaches seen in picture no.16 pass over the junction with the Dorking line. The near part of the yard is used by the Electrical Engineer and the distant part is occupied by Chipmans for their weed-killing trains. (J. Scrace)

72. There is only one station in West Sussex on the Dorking line, namely Warnham. It retained many LBSCR features but is now only served by a few peak hour services. No. 5816 runs in from Horsham, bound for Victoria, on 28th April 1989. (J. Scrace)

74. No. 47418 leaves Horsham with empty stock to form the 09.56 Gatwick Airport - Manchester on 27th February 1983. The reason for this unusual movement is given in caption no.66. The connection in the foreground is for EMU berthing. (J. Scrace)

73. The luxury VSOE coaches appeared again at Horsham on 16th April 1983 when they were used for a RCTS tour originating and finishing at Victoria, and travelling via Chichester and Romsey. The locomotives are nos. 73142 and 73129. (J. Scrace)

75. Chipmans meet about half of BR's weed killing requirements from their premises at Horsham. Until 1989, BR provided motive power for their trains but now Chipmans operate privately-owned nos. 20904 (left) and 20901 (right), seen being serviced on 29th May 1989. (P. G. Barnes)

76. The "Class 501 Farewell Tour" approaches Horsham, formed of units 152 and 180 on 11th May 1985. The tour was organised by the SEG and LCGB, whose members would not have appreciated the bars at the windows! (C. Wilson)

77. Class 508 units were often used on the Dorking route, as witnessed on 29th July 1983 as no. 508031 leaves Horsham for Waterloo. They were later transferred to Merseyside as 3-car sets, the fourth vehicle being retained for use in the class 455/7 units. The siding on the right serves a UKF depot for bagged fertiliser. (J. Scrace)

78. Class 47s appeared at Horsham on 3rd October 1972 when the 07.15 from Manchester terminated at Gatwick Airport, due to engineering works south of Three Bridges. No. 47488 stands alongside the electrified berthing sidings. (J. Scrace)

79. No. 47565 poses alongside nos. 7386 and 7375 of the 4VEP class on 8th January 1983. The class 47s weigh over 120 tonnes, compared with the 77 tonnes of the class 33 commonly used on the Arun Valley line. (J. Scrace)

80. Christs Hospital signal box continued to control semaphore signals and double up as a booking office throughout the 1980s. It is seen from the former Guildford line platforms in July 1986. (V. Mitchell)

81. Another 1986 view of Christs Hospital shows the buildings on the down platform which, until 1967, was an island platform. By 1989, most trains were stopping here again, except on Sundays. (V. Mitchell)

←

82. Billingshurst signal box is shown in 1981, by which tiime it had probably reached its century. It has survived to be painted incongruously in NSE colours. (E. Wilmshurst)

84. 4 SUB unit no. 4732 was selected for preservation and repainted in SR colours. It is seen on 26th February 1983 at Amberley, where the site of the goods yard (behind the down platform) has been transformed into a car park for the Chalk Pits Museum. (J. Scrace)

←

83. Apart from car park improvements, little has altered on the Arun Valley line in the decade. The signal boxes are therefore the most interesting operational feature to record. A permanent way engineer's siding has been retained at the former loop platform, where trains from Midhurst once terminated. (E. Wilmshurst)

85. The lean-to on the right houses a knee-frame, a now rare form of signal operation using very short levers. A Victoria to Littlehampton service slows down on 13th August 1984. (V. Mitchell)

86. No. 023 is one of three stores units which tour the depots weekly. Formerly a 2HAL unit, no. 023 was diverted through Amberley on 26th February 1983 owing to engineering works on the direct route between New Cross Gate and Brighton. (J. Scrace)

CLASS A - LANDSCAPE AND STATIONS

87. No. 33061 accelerates away from Arundel with the 11.26 Fratton to Waterloo parcels train on 29th December 1985, with Offham Quarry in the background. With its two castles, the Arun Valley is one of the best scenic railway routes in the south-east of England. (C. Wilson)

88. West Sussex County Council has been heavily involved in supporting the line, and on 12th December 1988 a special train was run from Crawley to Chichester, as part of the council's centenary celebrations. It is seen at Arundel with WSCC chairman, Mr Peter Shepherd, on the left. His brother, David, is the well known artist and locomotive owner. (J. Scrace)

89. The driver of the special train was F. Goff and he was accompanied by Inspector R. Cann. Only one train regularly uses the crossover at Arundel - the 08.08 departure for Chichester on Mondays to Fridays. (J. Scrace)

BRIGHTON MAIN LINE

90. Gatwick Airport has generated immense traffic for BR during the decade and the opening of an additional terminal on 26th April 1983, brought a new internal transport problem. It was solved by the use of two penumatic-tyred cars, guided by solid rubber tyres acting on a central vertical concrete rail. Control is automatic; power is 600 volts; speed is up to 22mph and 5000 passengers per hour can be carried. (Pamlin Prints)

91. No. 73211 *County of West Sussex* stands at Gatwick Airport with the 18.50 Gatwick Express to Victoria on 28th January 1989. At the other end of the fully air conditioned train would be a driving luggage van. This 15-minute interval service was introduced in May 1984. (C. Wilson)

92. The DLV is normally at the London end of a Gatwick Express but, on 11th May 1984, the reverse applied as a special working from Stewarts Lane to Brighton ran south. (J. Scrace)

93. Aircraft pass over the main line every few minutes and trains come and go at almost the same frequency. Departing south on 17th July 1983 is the 10.23 Manchester - Brighton service, hauled by no. 47482. In the right distance are sidings for berthing some terminating trains. (J. Scrace)

94. Part of the main airport building is visible as no. 73140 heads the 09.30 Salfords-Cliffe train of Bretts aggregate wagons. These electro-diesel locomotives have proved their versatility on so many different duties in the area. (J. Scrace)

96. Three Bridges is also the centre for permanent way work in the area, there being extensive yards both sides of the main line, south of the station. No. 33035 waits in the down yard at the head of a ballast train on 26th April 1984. Much track pre-assembly for the area takes place at this depot. (J. Scrace)

95. At Three Bridges, the signalling centre (right) has been expanded, since opening on 11th July 1983, to link up with the panels at Clapham Junction, London Bridge, Lewes, Lancing and Horsham on the main lines.   It contains seven adjoining panels, requiring a staff of that number during busy periods.
(C. N. Cheney)

97. The most interesting tour on the SR in 1987, motive power wise, was the "Three to the Sea" tour, which brought three class 20s from Sheffield to Brighton. Green 20064 and 20030 with Railfright 20118 pass Balcombe Tunnel Junction with the outward trip on 2nd May 1987. (C. Wilson)

98. No. 46026 *Leicestershire and Derbyshire Yeomanry* approaches the beginning of the quadruple track at Balcombe Tunnel Junction on 17th June 1984. It is heading a railtour to mark the demise of the class 46. It operated to and from Liverpool Street via the North London Line. (P. G. Barnes)

99. Balcombe Forest is the backdrop for this study of no. 73127 with an engineer's train. These locomotives develop 1420hp when operating electrically, but only 600hp on diesel power. (J. Petley)

101. A train from Brighton arrives at Balcombe on 26th June 1986 and passes under the lengthy road bridge. The station retained its separate building for gentlemen (left), so beloved by Victorian railway architects. (V. Mitchell)

100. No. 50023 *Howe* speeds south through Balcombe with an ADEX special from Oxford on 12th July 1986. This was the second locomotive of the class to receive NSE livery. (P. G. Barnes)

102. Nos. 20901 and 20904 bring Chipmans' weed killing train towards Haywards Heath on 28th May 1989. The line on the right leads to the Ardingly roadstone terminal and is used by trains of the type illustrated in picture no. 27. (P. G. Barnes)

104. In 1986-88, no less than four InterCity trains served the Brighton Line. The 06.35 Brighton-Manchester, headed by "Large Logo" no. 47646 and formed of a mixture of Blue and InterCity liveried stock emerges from Haywards Heath Tunnel on 10th June 1987. (J. Petley)

103. On 14th June 1988, no. 56062 overran signals, whilst hauling empty wagons from Ardingly, and rolled almost onto its roof, north of Haywards Heath. When photographed on 2nd October, sheet steel piling had been used to enable the bank to be cut back and the locomotive righted. The engine and alternator had been removed, ready for the body and bogies to be lifted individually later. (J. Scrace)

105. No. 73006 passes through Wivelsfield with the 15.36 Crawley New Yard - Newhaven on 5th September 1983. This working was later formed of more modern bogie wagons and ran from Tolworth. (J. Petley)

106. The 10.23 Manchester-Brighton, headed by no. 47545 and formed of air conditioned stock, passes Burgess Hill on 28th July 1983. The main station buildings are well above rail level here, and the corrugated covering to the long flight of steps down to the platform can be seen. All this had been scheduled for demolition. (J. Petley)

107. A stores unit passes through Burgess Hill on its way from Selhurst to Lovers Walk Depot at Brighton, on 17th September 1983. Plans were made for new station buildings on the site of the first ones, near the camera. (P. G. Barnes)

108. The 16.30 Redhill-Brighton parcels runs through Hassocks on 6th September 1983, hauled by no. 73113 (now named **County of West Sussex**). It was quite unusual to see so many vans. In 1988, this working started from London Bridge, and by 1989 it had been reduced to a single MLV-motor luggage van. (J. Petley)

109. Hassocks is seen at 16.21 on 24th April 1988. On Sundays a class 319 operated a stopping service between Brighton and Haywards Heath, where it connected with the Victoria-Portsmouth Harbour fast train. (C. Wilson)

110. 319013 was the first class 319 to reach Brighton and is seen here emerging from Clayton Tunnel on the return trip as the 11.16 Brighton to Selhurst Depot, on March 1st 1988. The pantograph on the second coach is used north of Farringdon, where AC current gives the units a better performance than that achieved on the DC conductor rail. (C. Wilson)

111. No. 33209 passes through the South Downs between Clayton and Patcham Tunnels, with a Bolton-Brighton Excursion on 12th May 1984. The train was over one hour late, giving the trippers a mere four hours by the sea before they had to begin their long journey north. (J. Petley)

113. Early days of the Manchester-Brighton trains: no. 47446 hauls a rake of Mk 1 coaches (forming the 07.27 from Manchester) near Lover's Walk (Brighton) on 9th September 1981. On the left is the former Pullman Car Works where the Southern Electric Group was to start work on the restoration of 4COR unit no. 3142 in 1986. The Cliftonville Spur, seen in picture no. 1, is behind the shed. (J. Petley)

112. No. 73101 *Brighton Evening Argus* is at the rear of a Gatwick Express set as it formed the 08.59 Brighton-Victoria on 13th April 1984. It is passing through Preston Park on a passenger evaluation trip. (J. Scrace)

114. Unit no. 7394 leaves Brighton on 9th May 1984 and gives us the opportunity to see the track layout before the major changes took place early in 1985. For most of April, all London trains were routed via Hove, where reversal was necessary. Platform lengthening and the rebuilding of the bridge over New England Road was included in the £134M scheme. (J. Scrace)

116. The 1882 train shed was extensively renovated in 1984, during "Operation New Look" and no. 9 platform (extreme left) lost its track during the alterations. No. 47106 waits to leave with a return excursion to Birmingham. (J. Petley)

115. A glimpse from a Coastway East train on 17th August 1989 shows some of the new trackwork laid during the upheavals of 1985. No. 319049 is standing in a berthing siding. The cliff face in the background was sprayed with cement by abseiling craftsmen during 1989. (V. Mitchell)

117. No. 73111 departs with the 17.59 vans to London Bridge, whilst green-liveried 47484 **Isambard Kingdom Brunel** awaits departure with the 18.26 to Liverpool on 13th May 1986. The space occupied by the signal box was incorporated into the car park, all train movements being controlled from Three Bridges. (J. S. Petley)

118. Introduced in 1959, the ten MLVs were used almost exclusively with Kent coast boat trains until the late 1980s. Their liveries now include NSE and Royal Mail red - this example was loading mail bags at platform 7 at Brighton on 17th August 1989. (V. Mitchell)

119.   Photographed from an unusual angle in 1988, Brighton station retains its original facade, with its later porte-cochere and carriage road built out over Trafalgar Street. (A. C. Mott)

120.   To finish with a smile.   In 1989, **Steam Railway** carried a feature on inaccurate railway inn signs but failed to include this gem, which replaced an **accurate** one in 1988.   The location is half a mile south of Chichester station. (V. Mitchell)

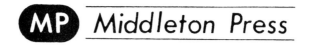

Easebourne Lane, Midhurst. West Sussex. GU29 9AZ
(0730) 813169

BRANCH LINES

BRANCH LINES TO MIDURST
BRANCH LINES AROUND MIDHURST
BRANCH LINES TO HORSHAM
BRANCH LINES TO ALTON
BRANCH LINE TO HAYLING
BRANCH LINE TO SOUTHWOLD
BRANCH LINE TO TENTERDEN
BRANCH LINES TO NEWPORT
BRANCH LINES TO TUNBRIDGE WELLS
BRANCH LINE TO SWANAGE
BRANCH LINES TO LONGMOOR
BRANCH LINE TO LYME REGIS
BRANCH LINE TO FAIRFORD
BRANCH LINE TO ALLHALLOWS
BRANCH LINES AROUND ASCOT
BRANCH LINES AROUND WEYMOUTH
BRANCH LINE TO HAWKHURST

SOUTH COAST RAILWAYS

CHICHESTER TO PORTSMOUTH
BRIGHTON TO EASTBOURNE
RYDE TO VENTNOR
EASTBOURNE TO HASTINGS
PORTSMOUTH TO SOUTHAMPTON
SOUTHAMPTON TO BOURNEMOUTH
ASHFORD TO DOVER
BOURNEMOUTH TO WEYMOUTH

SOUTHERN MAIN LINES

WOKING TO PORTSMOUTH
HAYWARDS HEATH TO SEAFORD
EPSOM TO HORSHAM
CRAWLEY TO LITTLEHAMPTON
THREE BRIDGES TO BRIGHTON
WATERLOO TO WOKING
VICTORIA TO EAST CROYDON
TONBRIDGE TO HASTINGS
EAST CROYDON TO THREE BRIDGES
WOKING TO SOUTHAMPTON
WATERLOO TO WINDSOR
LONDON BRIDGE TO EAST CROYDON

COUNTRY RAILWAY ROUTES

BOURNEMOUTH TO EVERCREECH JNCT
READING TO GUILDFORD
WOKING TO ALTON
BATH TO EVERCREECH JUNCTION
GUILDFORD TO REDHILL
EAST KENT LIGHT RAILWAY
FAREHAM TO SALISBURY
BURNHAM TO EVERCREECH JUNCTION

STEAMING THROUGH

STEAMING THROUGH KENT
STEAMING THROUGH EAST HANTS
STEAMING THROUGH SURREY
STEAMING THROUGH WEST SUSSEX
STEAMING THROUGH THE ISLE OF WIGHT
STEAMING THROUGH WEST HANTS

OTHER RAILWAY BOOKS

WAR ON THE LINE
GARRAWAY FATHER & SON
LONDON CHATHAM & DOVER RAILWAY
INDUSTRIAL RAILWAYS OF THE S. EAST
WEST SUSSEX RAILWAYS IN THE 1980S

OTHER BOOKS

MIDHURST TOWN THEN & NOW
EAST GRINSTEAD THEN & NOW

WALKS IN THE WESTERN HIGH WEALD

MILITARY DEFENCE OF WEST SUSSEX
SUSSEX POLICE FORCES

WEST SUSSEX WATERWAYS
SURREY WATERWAYS
KENT AND EAST SUSSEX WATERWAYS